# The Glass Aisle

*for Steph*

# The Glass Aisle
*Paul Henry*

Seren is the book imprint of
Poetry Wales Press Ltd.
57 Nolton Street, Bridgend, Wales, CF31 3AE
www.serenbooks.com
facebook.com/SerenBooks
twitter@SerenBooks

The right of Paul Henry to be identified as
the author of this work has been asserted in accordance
with the Copyright, Designs and Patents Act, 1988.

© Paul Henry, 2018

ISBN: 978-1-78172-440-8
ebook: 978-1-78172-441-5
Kindle: 978-1-78172-442-2

A CIP record for this title is available from the British Library.

The publisher acknowledges the financial assistance of the Welsh Books Council.

Cover painting: 'View from a Canal Bridge'
by Simon Palmer. Simon Palmer is represented
by Portland Gallery www.portlandgallery.com

Printed by Airdrie Print Services Ltd.

# Contents

# I

## The Hesitant Song

# Cliff Terrace Clouds

The summer's clouds are moving east.
My father stokes their fires.

They do not know it is winter,
that I am already old.

Over the Sugarloaf they go,
full of my mother's songs.

Over the hill's white pebbles,
away, away from the sea.

# Last of the Sixties Mothers

Waves curl up the estate,
her wild strands in the wind.

Anchored by her balcony gate
she holds her highest ground,

the jetsam of her decade
beached on suburban drives –

a dish-rack of forty-fives,
melamine picnic plates,

starburst clocks, half-alive,
shrivelled inflatable chairs...

She calls out our names
in case we are still here,

our satchel bells in the wind,
our buckled sandal-chimes

rising up the pavement
on the afternoon tide.

# The Hesitant Song

*... And when she sang, the sea*
*Whatever self it had, became the self*
*That was her song...*

Wallace Stevens – 'The Idea of Order at Key West'

*I*

These chords I barely hear
breaking over the bay
I think it is Catrin Sands

in a gale, spinning them
with creaturely hands
out of a wild sea

but sending them here
*pianissimo,*
to comfort me.

(I moved into silence
then silence moved into me.

My father locked the music room
and threw away the key.)

★

Inside the sun's amber arcade,
a beat before the singer sings

the sea's soft pedal

the harbour bell

the baton hovering

                    the bow
half-touching its string

a beat before the singer sings.

★

Inside the piano's grain
my mother's songs turn bright,
diminish, brighten again –

*Senza Mamma, Dove Sono,
Ave Maria, Porgi amor...*


II

Dear Catrin Sands, Cat,
the same sea song
broke inside us

inside the piano's grain.

We closed our eyes
and the chapels set sail.

It happens in a beat,
the flight of hands

and Cat, I cannot,
except by her voice,
be saved.

★

Inside the stained glass,
its amber arcades

time angles for shadows
our ancestors saw –

that wing-flit over the pulpit,
across the pews

now high enough
to kiss the sky's keel.

★

Paws in our ears
the children we were

thunder over staves
to the sea and do not hear

on a platform's blur
her song in the leaves

growing louder.

Summer on summer,
before we arrive
and after we leave,

the leadlight rose
inside the heart
on *Penllain*'s glass

is trying, Cat, to open.

★

*Pianissimo*, Catrin Sands,
to comfort me.

After the flight of hands
the sea's soft pedal

the baton hovering

     the bow
half-touching its string

a beat before the singer sings.

*III*

Dear, jilted *Sao Ohn Nyunt*,
my mother hated you,
the distance in your eyes,

the worried silk of your tail,
your serenity in despair.

Above broken strings,
slammed doors,
an oboe's Himalayan scales…

you waited on this wall
for your hand to be held,
for the music to end.

And now that it has
we can hear.

★

To orchestrate silence:

tilt the harp's heirloom
stage-left of the grate
into its alcove, so

then put your foot through it

put your foot through it

your foot through it

foot through it

through it

.

★

Under the dark *Steinway*,
the sea's absence
flooded the room each day.

And I might still be there
listening to the bay,
but for the sea's returning

to bear her songs away.


*IV*

Cat, our singer's house
threw a party last night.

Geta wore her wedding hat,
Edith Smart played Mozart.

The piano's wax lighthouse
haunted the glazed bay –

first to light the frame
at the first beat of time.

And Cat, it was hard to say
where the sea met the sky.

★

My dark-eyed ghost,
my page turner,

stay inside this rest.
A lullaby drips

into your darkness,
kisses your fingertips.

Your breath that lifts
this leaf from its dust
belongs to a lost coast,

its ebb of prayers,
its waves' creases
in a beach dress.

Stay inside this rest,
or put on the sea,
the song transposed.

★

The sea's soft pedal –
a rumour we were here.

The pillow's crater terrifies,
its print of a scream.

Its lunar stillness
holds the weight of dreams.

Then in the empty house all day
it is the dune where we played

inside the sun's amber arcade.

★

Inside the sun's amber arcade
her songs diminish, brighten again –

*Senza Mamma, Dove Sono,
Ave Maria, Porgi amor...*

Inside the piano's grain

the sea's soft pedal

the baton hovering

                           the bow
half-touching its string

a beat before the singer sings.

## Put on the Sun

Put on the sun, Catrin Sands, your yellow dress
ten winters in darkness
in Geta's wardrobe, the sun that taps to be let out
when the door clicks shut
and its mirror spies, upright in bed, Geta's ghost
inside a twirl of dust
with Enoch's bible, her shotgun, her *Cambrian News*.

All the terrace windows
turn gold when you wear it, the summer has begun.
Put on the sun
Catrin Sands, let's walk behind our shadows
on the promenade of sighs.

# Craiglais

*for Will Troughton*

Here is the tunnel in the cliff,
the wormhole between coves

we dare to crawl through
when the tide is high,

sensing it might disappear
in a stone's cry

           and here

is the other, brighter side,
another planet, a lower tide.

The sea is that far away
we cannot see its claws

crawling through pebbles
patiently, towards us.

# The Violin

I dreamt it was not yours
but Mengele's violin,
wrapped like a brittle child

in a white, municipal shawl,
laid in a cradle's mould
in a hospital ward.

I traced the cracks in its grain,
the fiddleback, finger board
ribs, waist, hourglass,

the purfled head, neck,
pegbox, tail, rest,
the soul's tilted sound post…

then I saw you, laid out
for silence, its frail bridge
to the stars, no air

to augment the final slur,
your cast of a note exhaled.
Then love, pity and shame

were raw as the early sky
void of cadenzas,
reels, jigs, lullabies.

# Dwynwen

*Surdus. Larus
religiosus.*

Ashen mac,
pebbly specs.

Blood-red bill
with china tip.

Shrill call –
*dacw-it, dacw-it…*

Last sighted
in '64

stealing a nap
on Aber pier.

# The Sea in Pieces

Prydwen Jane, glass palaces
at the end of Gorseflower Lane
are bright with familiar rooms.
Their windows blaze in the sun.
Their light that held the future
holds the past. Louder
with each step, their panes
break in precious pieces
on the sand. With each step
a year younger, Prydwen Jane.

They wait for you in the glare.
Keep your sunglasses on.
A fanfare of gulls, brass light
deafens on the shore.
Here they are, Bet and Dai
and little Nest on the blanket.
A crab makes a violin of itself.
Was the sand ever this warm,
Prydwen Jane? Their arms
rise as one, to wave at you.

# Brown Helen Reclining

Nothing wakes her,
not the wind's stammer
snagged on a gate

nor the ticking as I wind
a new line onto my reel.

The stripes on her deckchair
go blue-orange-blue…

*Penllain*'s cracked patio
aspires to a yacht.

I have not yet kissed
her closed eyes.

I miss her too easily,
the hook in her smile.

The sun catches her now
with an earring.

                    One sigh.
A summer has passed.

And where she swims
in what she dreams
is further out to sea

than any line I cast.

# The Fireplace

No one's in except the sea.
Geta's on the Aber bus
to fix her teeth again, Catrin's
too far out to see her fin.
Is that you, Brown Helen?
I'll make a fire, shall I?

*Penllain*'s out of season,
a vitrine of embers.
I come here when it's empty,
to listen out for you,
your laughter in the walls

to press the shingly bell
before I turn the key and push
into the sandy vestibule.

What is it in you, Helen
rakes me back to this ingle,
its firedogs and clock
anchored in '69,
its bellows' dusty gills?

*And my teeth went CRACK!*

A vacant shell still hears.
Come closer to the chimney,
its song to our ears

or is it our mothers
mistaken for the sea?

The bunker's wood is dry.
Helen, it's almost late.
Geta's smile returns
to a kitchen knocked through.
Catrin moors *Gwyneth Blue*
on a new skylight window.

I'll draw these flames to heel.
Your chair is too far away.
The bay is rising now.
Warm your hands on its light.

Tell me you can feel
all our summers in this grate.

# The Wicker Gondola

Down it goes,
where builders found a river
in the ruins of light.

Set sail in a half-built estate
waiting for bricks, children,
the sun's plasterer...

down it goes to the sea.

# II

## The Glass Aisle

# The Glass Aisle

*Through the telephone wires, a wilderness of voices*
*Blown for a thousand miles, for a hundred years...*

James Wright – 'Listening to the Mourners'


The line to the old workhouse is down.
The telegraph pole is caged in a tree,
the engineer wedged like a sacrifice
inside the branch's lattice-work.

The sun puts a match to him,
his luminous goggles, his helmet's
white bud twitching to birdsong.

The workhouse waits across the canal.
He has been up there for hours,
too high to engage in small talk
as he strains to hear lost voices –

*Abraham Bishop, Pauper, Gloucester*
*Charlot Phillips, Wife, Carmarthen*
*Easau Daly, Tailor, Ireland...*


★


I wanted to know their names
but the sign by the Union bridge
read *Please Respect the Privacy*
*of Residents*

                and though we carve
the names of war and love,
perhaps their voices were enough –

on the bank, in the steep lanes,
under bridges where faces peered
through crumbling mortar...


29

*Sam Hawkes, Groom, Wiltshire*
*Jane Price, Unknown, Brynmawr…*

Some nights they kept me awake,
small brooks whispered in the walls,
too many at once, so I couldn't tell

a story from a prayer,
an owl from a name on the wind.

★

The dandelion hours drift like snow
across the hooded, sunlit canal

light and aimless in their flight…

*Mary Thomas, Inmate, Llandysul…*

*When my boy cried in chapel*
*they sent me to the Master's room…*

between the workhouse and the bridge.

*He put one hand on my neck,*
*the other under my clothes.*
*When I told him No, he kicked me…*

The canal is inside me now.
Its arches rig my spine.

*Ordered me to Merthyr.*
*The night before they came*
*no one saw a woman and child…*

Soon I'll not turn back.

*disappear into an arch,*
*while there was still light.*

★

I climb up Folly Lane
then down to where the woods
grow deep into the mirrored sky.

The towpath is profligate
with primroses, deadnettle, willow…
Moorhens trail their sunlight.

Whose face peers into me?

*John Moonlight, Angler, Crickhowell…*

★

John Moonlight, your name
is fading from its bench.

Three bulls on the other bank
drink from its reflection.

The sun in the water.
The bridge that likes butter.

Children camp in the field
where you hid your night-lines.
A breeze plays with their laughter.

The hill's frown softens
over the tramway they cut
to bring down the lime –

*Rees Jones, Ffawyddog,*
*'crushed by a tram'*

*Edward Bevan, Pant-y-rhiw,*
*'crushed by a tram'*

*William Morgan, White Wall,*
*'crushed by a rock-fall'...*

The sated bulls retreat
into the tall bracken.

The sun in the water.
The bridge that likes butter...

John, if I may, whose laughter
was writ in air,
whose moment the sun engraves,

*who loved this view,*

something of your ecstasy survives.

★

The wind picks at it,
water feature of its past,
stapled to the land.

An arch makes a moon
that cows amble over
and O it is tame.

           A river
snuck under a town
and spawned it

and sometimes it knows,
a finch on a twig
surfs the hint of a wave

a duck's wake widens

to a forgery of the sea.

★

What summer houses did they build?
Slated in leaves
all their roofs are still.

*John Rosel, Tinker, Carmarthen*
*George Butcher, Weaver, Frome*
*James Grant, Seaman, Boston...*

★

A gale's sledge hammer
shocks the high summer leaves.
Picks, chisels, crow bars...

The inmates have turned –
skin-peelers, rope-pickers,
prayer-darners, stone-breakers...

Ushered over by the wind
their voices in the trees

*Richard Warr, Tailor, Dymock*
*John James, Puddler, Neath...*

cross the canal's border
in dialects of green: Alder
Ash, Oak, Birch...

The sun touches each leaf
as if it were the first
to sing, to open its wings.

Each nib's calligraphy
scratches in air, then on stone

*I was never so free.*

★

Where a bridge was, two boughs touch,
to close an absence,
keeping autumn's sough to themselves.

★

Earlier, on the towpath
I stood to one side to let him pass,

my son, on his blue bike,
speeding through a bridge's arch –

his hair darker, his *Thanks* deeper
as he rode away from me

into the leaf shower.

★

Each leaf must fall,
some to the bank,
some to the water

the one that clings
and the one that lets go

the one that hides a song,
the one that flirts
with a sneezing wind

the one that grows
beyond itself, its pallor
a ghost of green.

Each leaf must fall,
crazy paving
the canal's cellar...

while inside his branches
the engineer curses
the workhouse line,

his red beard longer,
his eyes on fire,
his skull a full cemetery –

*Bridget Skeyne, Pauper, Ireland*
*John Nickhols, Innkeeper, Scotland...*

★

Mary, some nights I see you

between the giant redwood and the kilns,
half-immersed – Millais' *Ophelia* –
the summer's flowers in your outstretched hand.

I stop and think I hear a woman's voice
inside the reeds, at the wilder bend
where a river passes under the canal

until words become water again,
and I move on, along the darkening aisle.

How did your colours find me?

A late boat moors, its farrier's ghost
hammering steel pegs into the night.

★

*Dreamcatcher* is listing.
Someone gave her captain a book too many.
Her ropes droop but keep her moored.
Perhaps it was Villon tipped the balance,
or was it Verlaine.

                              Anyway, he's left
for a wider bed, weary with warming hands
on candles, weary with owls
and the stench of diesel, with the winter's
long tunnel.

                        *Dreamcatcher* is listing,
held by the starry ice until he returns.


                              ★


John Moonlight walked it
when it froze, the glass aisle,
walked on water
between Glanusk and Heron's Rest.

John Moonlight, whose loves
he left at Fourteen Locks.

Winters fractured in his wake.
The small stove at his lips
shrouded him in smoke
as he passed through arches

as if rehearsing his spirit.

Then a new year's ice
lost patience with his weight.

*The water came up to his heart...*

*The cold. He cradled his head...*

*The star still burned in his pipe...*

And in his eyes... not terror
but disbelief, that it could give
beneath him, as they cheered –

*William Wall, Vagrant, Hanley*
*Tom Powell, Idiot, Meirionydd...*

★

Hushed in lofty nests
they wait – Sutherland, Callas,
de los Ángeles...

*Marg Jones, Servant, Cardigan*
*Becca James, Servant, Cwmdu*
*Harriet Morris, Servant, Llangattock...*

★

Half-wool, half-air,
small gods, their sphere
a foot above the earth,
the lambs at bridge 114

all calling for the mayor.

★

Mary's here, on a white horse
drenched in medieval leaflight.
I am not dreaming this.

★

The telegraph pole is caged in a tree,
the engineer wedged like a sacrifice
inside the branch's lattice-work.

He has been up there for a year,
too high to engage in small talk
as he strains to hear lost voices –

*Will Solsbury, Miner, Somerset*
*Lizzie Lewis, Pauper, Llanelli...*

Saplings, primed like rockets
in their tubes, wait for their fuse.

The workhouse waits on its wire.

★

Inside the canal's cathedral,
its screens' arabesque,
Byrd and Tallis sing. Let us
gasp at the heron's lectern,
its neck's dark tunnel
a fish slips into,
thinking it leads to the sea.
Let us praise bright polyphony
needling through glass,
the kingfisher in summer
flying with its twin in the pane.

★

Towed by younger men on the path
a flat-capped elder in tweeds
inspects the overhanging trees

balances on a raft.

Birdsong is in full bloom.
Branches spread their hands
as if to hold a stillness in place.

Shadow man on a laurel,
on a pillar laced with squirrels,
his sons are men, his river a canal.

He kneels, leans over
and stares, old Narcissus.

A woman stares back,
tries to speak, disappears.

The green, cavernous years
echo with her voice.

The field's cob laughs at him,
too engrossed at the Union bridge

to see the scarecrow engineer,
to hear the roll-call crossing the wire –

*Emily Jeffreys, Seamstress, Ebbw Vale...*

★

None but the workhouse muses –

*Jane Thomas, Unknown, St Clears
Jane Williams, Unknown, Unknown...*

sees flayed Marsyas, nailed to his pole.

★

I'll walk you to the bridge, Mary
where we sheltered from the years.
Along infinite cloisters
I'll walk you with rain in our eyes
to the village sleeping in its blur
and the bridge with small brooks
in its walls.

        From rusty vaulting
drip the syllables of prayer.
The act of sheltering is enough.
Clouds clear, stars spill,
cows amble over the moon.

*Dreamcatcher* is listing.
I cannot tell an owl
from a name on the wind,
the voices in the wire
from the voices in the leaves.

Each nib's calligraphy
scratches on stone, on glass, in air

*I was never so free.*

# The Seamstress

As if she might still save
the trees from themselves
on the towpath, my wife
is pinning back the leaves.

And for every leaf returned
another falls to the ground,
to the colours of heartbreak,
of clothes she used to make.

From oak to beech to aspen
she carries her box of thorns.
The branches dance above her.
There are leaves in her hair.

Blood has dyed her fingers.
She does not see me here
as the colours rise and spin
with us inside them again.

And for every hour returned
another falls to the ground,
to the colours of heartbreak,
of clothes she used to make.

# Green Man Walking

Gary, I'm walking back to the village
along the canal. I'm at the half-way bridge
where the cars do a shimmy then straighten again
leaving us behind. I'll get home soon.

I just saw our fathers leap. Get Lynne to read this
or Jan, or Sally, or Bron y Llan, or Jess.
Tell them about the Green Man, his noise
inside the canal's green light, how the boys
will meet them here if they want to dance.

And tell them, Gary, how the water dances
and leaps in us still – away from the Green Man
who is quieter now – how it dances on stone
with the sunlight, under the half-way bridge
as I walk back to the village.

# Festival Field

The deafened owl will soon return
and birdsong, to its stages in air.
Did I dream you were here?
Your footprints fill with rain.

Your tightly packed rucksack,
the daisy crown in your hair
weight and levitate an hour
dazed in sunlight. If you came back

to hold court on these hay bales,
a summer's ruins, to tell me
who you were, are and shall be
under the sky's torn sails

I might sleep more easily,
let centuries plough over me.

# Naming the Cast

*i.m. Derek Prosser*

Still dangerous in his chair
he is naming the village cast –

*Charlie Hasam, Sharky Price,*
*Nancy, the Cawleys, Jack Buail...*

Against no breeze to speak of
the window's field is trying to breathe.

*Siân Meredith, Billy Griff,*
*Arthur Rhydderch, Linda Games...*

Buried deep in his lungs, a scythe
waits to be found.

                    *Ginger Mair,*
*Syd Bowen, Yank, Emmy, Stahl...*

Only three to go: the strongman,
the clown and the pantomime dame.

He clenches and unclenches his fist
for a name, a name, a name...

III

# Shelves

The old books are the last to leave,
from alcoves either side of the fire
into gaping carrier bags,
their titles, their ordered lives
a haul of slithering fish.
Bookmarks: letters, photographs
of the boys… slip free
like spilt playing cards, like knives.

And how will they survive,
the souls of our marriage,
in a flat without shelves,
in blocks that sway and fall?
Like ancient stones disturbed by war
they had become their walls.

# The Father in the Well

Can you hear him, boys?
Who put him in?
There are mice and bats
inside the wall's ring.

Some nights he cannot bear
to hear your laughter spill
from the moonlit porthole

into his tower in the ground.
He covers his furry ears
and pretends he did not fall.
Then he digs and finds

the key to a lost house,
three plastic bracelets
with your misspelt names, cut
where they can't be joined again.

Boys, something deeper
must have been at play.
*Ding-dong bell…*

The bats and the mice
go round and round.
The moon wears a starry chain.

# Grove Park

Kathy, when I bought my first tie
and loosened it at five each day
for a stranger outstaring me
on the underground, you took me in
and your name was home.

                   The Thames
loosened its knots yards from your door.
Your hall light offered a flame
to the watery dark.

              A tunnel's rumour
grew louder, its breath colder...
Then the city remembered its name.
*Kathy*, it whispered, deep in its lines.

# The White-leaved Oak

Have we not longed for a simpler love
where silence lays its infinite fields
around what is left unsaid,
where the bells in the branches are enough?

We touch fingers, to pen cumuli.
The oak has known us for centuries.
We lie down in its shade, kiss and die,
kiss and die...

# St Michael's

The rivers of our childhoods find us here.
Through cages in the earth they pour
and we rise, venture out

in all our ages, gingerly at first,
following our seasons home
along their bright aisles.

It is winter and the orchards are bare.

A blackcap outsings a name on stone,
the lullaby inside a hymn,
the clock and the bells.

★

After the ice has held the river's breath
a different creature swims on
over the worn cobbles

making for the sea, another Leadon,
Lugg, Dore, Monnow, Wye...
song without end.

It is spring and plastic bonnets in the wind

give perms a holy glow, under the yew,
beside the stone keyholes
we can't peer through.

★

Dry inside the spaces between the rain,
its cider chimes, we drift
down Church Lane

carrying our apples, *Wizards*, gas masks,
our picnic blankets, tartan flasks,
our hoops and cricket bats.

It is summer and the rivers have no names.

In the parish of a bird's song, without coats
we follow our seasons home
along their bright aisles.

## Lockyer's

The door's cowbell, tall Cyril
ushering, his own bookmark
between 'Roses' and 'Churchill',
the fey assistant's Bakelite...

The floorboards creaked in 'Poetry'.
A branch scratched the skylight.

I could hear my sons in the park,
sometimes recognised a cry,
a soul's baroque lattice-work
annotating *The Waste Land*.

The books we almost bought
were precious in our hands –

Keyes's *The Iron Laurel*,
a pocket Tennyson, inscribed
*For Olive, before I sail...*

Weekends turned, chimed.
The boys grew tall enough
to panic a cowbell, drag me home

as Mr Lockyer's century closed
on a park's empty shelves,
a room full of leaves.

# Windfalls

The trees are the wind's maypoles.
Their rags jingle with apples –

*Old Bromley*

       *Lord Hindlip*

*Stoke Edith*

       *Cwmmy Crab...*

I drink to them, in stained glass,
their windfall of centuries –

*Bran Rose*

       *Doctor Hare's*

*Gennet Moyle*

       *Eggleton Styre...*

O beaded air of Marcle Ridge
in a jar! O Weston's Vintage!

*Wormsley Pippin*

       *Handsome Norman*

*Kingston Black*

       *Cherry Permain...*

Once upon a tree, a fallen kiss.

# Blunt Razor

Your shaving mirror cuts,
a steel, concertina affair
that reaches in and out of the wall
like a clown's boxing glove –
the legacy of a practical man.

I gaze into its misted sphere
and see you there,
rough-shaven, head in hands,
plotting my end.

I think I know your room,
its haunted bed,
the filigree of ice on the pane,
the wallpaper's grouse motif
repeating its din in the gloom...

I think I know your wounds,

the edge of an old blade
through winter fields.

# Chainsaws in the Mist

Another man's scream
tries to cut a way out.

His house has disappeared.
So much for boundaries.

He lives alone like me,
on the other side of this field.

Once we had families,
doors creaked in the trees.

Across the white silence
our chainsaws scream.

# The *STOP* and *GO* Man

Today my donkey-jacket turned bright,
outshone their headlights.

I did not move so easily. Not mine
but another man's bones
creaked inside the polyester.

In caves beneath their cars
the centuries ground their gears.

Sheep ignored the star
over the last field to the sea.
Leaves danced about the queue
snaking back for miles.

And they bowed to me, at their wheels –
teachers, loan sharks, fishermen,
farmers, priests, publicans…

as if my sign's giant key
could turn a planet's misery
on its axis, from red to green.
What brightness had they seen?

The longer they waited, the less I knew.
One wound down her window –

*What are we queueing for?*
I made up an answer –
*To feel the sea wind on your skin.*

Then inside a dazzle I spun the sign
and let the dead leaves through,
and let the dead leaves through…

# The Nettle Race

Tilting into the garden wall
three boys' bicycles,
frieze of an abandoned race.

Briars cover the chains,
their absent riders' chins.
The tortoise rust won with ease.

Slowly the sun leans
towards its finishing line.

# Not Stopping

Unable to visit you, down the line
I waited at the station for your train –
with all the other songs and scenes –
gave a wave as you sped through,
hoping the gesture might serve,
that, inside the moment, you'd believe
you had seen your old man wave
as if in a dream, as you sped through

and that this would be enough,
accepting good men and bad men
share the same name, and that love
however distant along its track,
however brief its glance, can forgive,
wave back.

# Acknowledgements

Some of these poems first appeared in the following journals and anthologies:

*Ambit*, *'Hwaet!'* (Bloodaxe, ed. Mark Fisher), *New Welsh Review*, *'Off the Shelf'* (Picador, ed. Carol Ann Duffy), *Planet*, *Poetry Ireland Review*, *Poetry Wales*, *The Spectator*, *The Times Literary Supplement*.

'St Michael's' was commissioned by Feral Productions for the 2017 Ledbury Poetry Festival. The names in 'Windfalls' are Herefordshire apples.

The book's title-poem evolved from an Arts Council of Wales 'Creative Wales Award' and is set on a stretch of canal above Crickhowell. I am grateful to the Rev. Margaret Williams whose pamphlet, *The Spike*, includes the story of Mary Thomas and an 1840s census in which the poem's names appear.

A performance version of 'The Glass Aisle', including songs co-written with Brian Briggs (stornoway.eu/), was touring at the time of publication (@theglassaisle). I am grateful to Becky Fincham for making this happen.

The collection's completion was aided by a *Literature Wales* Writer's Bursary which was funded by the National Lottery through the Arts Council of Wales.

For their scrutiny of the poems, thanks are due to Stephen Knight, Jane Houston, Carolyn Sally Jones and to my editor, Amy Wack.

## Author Note

Paul Henry was born in Aberystwyth. His previous books include the best-selling *The Brittle Sea: New and Selected Poems*. A Writing Fellow at the University of South Wales, he's presented programmes for BBC Radio Wales, Radio 3 and Radio 4. Also a singer-songwriter, the author has performed his work at festivals in Europe, Asia and the USA.